POET'S ENGLAND 19

DORSET

Compiled by Guy Stapleton

Illustrated by Peter Durrant

Brentham Press

First published 1996 by
Brentham Press, 40 Oswald Road, St Albans, Herts AL1 3AQ

ISBN 0 905772 49 0

British Library Cataloguing-in-Publication Data
A catalogue record this book is available from the British Library

DTP by Gillian Durrant
Printed in England by Watkiss Studios Ltd, Biggleswade, Beds SG18 9ST

FOREWORD

Dorset is a multi-faceted jewel of a county. Its diamond shape holds within it the fertile clay vales of the north, the solitude of Cranborne Chase and the central ridge of chalk downland, and the southern lowland of little river valleys and sandy heathlands, terminating in its amazingly diverse coastline. This runs from the sands and cliffs of Bournemouth to the expanse of marshy creeks around Poole and the chalk and rugged cliffs of Purbeck, the bold headlands and secluded coves up to the sands of Weymouth Bay and the limestone mass of Portland, the long pebble ridge of the Chesil Bank and the vari-coloured cliffs around Lyme Regis.

It is essentially an agricultural county, with tourism, fishing and quarries also major contributors to the county's economy. But Dorset is especially rich in history. Such prehistoric remains as Maiden Castle, the Cerne Abbas giant, the camp on Eggardon and Badbury Rings have inspired contributors to this volume, as have the ruins of Corfe Castle, the wealth of major houses such as Athelhampton Hall, and Dorset's attractive market towns, as well as events such as the Tolpuddle Martyrs and the impact on the county of the Second World War and subsequent development.

Dorset's poetical history before the nineteenth century is a succession of comparatively minor figures: the Elizabethan epigrammatist Thomas Bastard and eighteenth century figures like Christopher Pitt and William Crowe, who all appear here, are not unrepresentative. Tastes in landscape differed then, of course; Robert Southey was perhaps speaking for many of the time when he described the Dorset Heights as a "dreary country"! But with the nineteenth and early twentieth century came Dorset's poetical glory: the gentle observation of William Barnes and the bleak though towering vision of Thomas Hardy, who in their turn inspired many later writers. Before the war poets in the Powys circle around Chaldon Herring also produced much work rooted in the local landscape, while many leading post-war poets have been led to write of the county.

Selecting from this rich vein has been a difficult though absorbing task, one which has been made even more pleasant and rewarding by the generosity of so many poets writing in and about Dorset today. They show that, after is comparatively late flowering here, poetry remains very much a living force in this most beautiful of counties.

November 1995   *Guy Stapleton*

ACKNOWLEDGMENTS

Thanks are especially due to R.G. Gregory of Word and Action (Dorset) Publications and Douglas Forward for introductions, helpful suggestions and provision of source material. Previous anthologies such as *Wessex Song* (Fowler Wright, 1928), *The Dorset Bedside Anthology* (Arundel Press, 1951) and *Poems on Hardy and Dorset* (Wanda, 1978) have also been very useful.

For the use of copyright material acknowledgment is made to:
The author and Dorset Publishing Co for "T.E. Lawrence's Grave at Moreton' by Neil Adams from *The Cobb and other Poems* (1991); Carcanet Press Ltd for 'On the Cobb at Lyme' by Patricia Beer from *Collected Poems* (1988) and 'Dorset' by Donald Davie from *The Shires* (1974); *The Countryman* for 'The Return of the Native' by H.M.G. Bond; Dobson Books for 'A Song of Loders' by Leonard Clark from *Singing in the Streets* (1972); Bloodaxe Books Ltd for 'Daybreak in Dorset' by Jack Clemo from *Selected Poems* (1988); Eleanor Farjeon Literary Estate for 'The Chimes of Cattistock' by Eleanor Farjeon from *A Collection of Poems* (1929); the author for 'Abbey Walk' by Ann Ford from *Caterpillar Wood and other Poems* (1980); The Society of Dorset Men for 'Abbotsbury Garland Day' by Olive M. Philpott from *The Dorset Year Book* (1960-61) and 'Cattistocky' by S. John Forrest from *The Dorset Year Book* (1978); John Murray for 'Sunday Evening at Studland Bay' by Lord Gorell from *Poems 1904-1936* (1937); the author and the *Daily Telegraph* for 'Requiem for Dorchester West' by Kenneth Leigh; the author and White Lion Press for 'Nature Reserve, Dorset' by Randle Manwaring from *Crossroads of the Year* (1975); the author and Peterloo Poets for 'Dinosaur Footprints Unearthed in Swanage' by Gerda Mayer from *A Heartache of Grass* (1988); Hamish Hamilton for 'Memory of England – October 1940' by Edna St Vincent Millay from *Make Bright the Arrows* (1941); St Catherine Press for 'Hill Forts of Dorset' by George Montagu Earl of Sandwich from *Gleanings* (1955); André Deutsch Ltd for 'Paradise for Sale' by Ogden Nash from *I Wouldn't Have Missed It* (1962); the author for 'West Bexington on Sea' by Mike Read from *Elizabethan Dragonflies* (1988); Ruislip Press for 'Old Dorset Women and Tanks' by Theodora Roscoe from *From the Chilterns* (1946); Methuen for 'The Martins Chapel' by Clive Sansom from *The Cathedral* (1958); the estate of Andrew Young for 'A Prehistoric Camp' from *The Poetical Works of Andrew Young*, ed. Lowbury & Young (Secker & Warburg, 1985).

Every effort has been made to trace copyright holders; any omission will be rectified if notified. Special thanks are due to all the poets who have provided previously published or new work for this anthology; copyright remains with the authors.

Poems are dated by the first year of publication where this is known.

CONTENTS

DORSET: Map showing main places mentioned in the text

DORSET

From Durlston Head to Blandford,
From Poole to Portland Bill,
And all the little villages
Round Shaston on its hill –
This is the land of Hardy, of Jude and Joseph Poorgrass,
     of Fancy Day the frolic, and tragic D'Urberville.

From Ilchester to Wimborne
(How sweet the Minster chime!),
And all the luscious pasturage
From Gillingham to Lyme –
This is the land of butter, the finest fairy butter, the famous
     "Dosset" butter, and butter all the time.

1926   *E.V. Lucas*

from
A JOURNEY TO EXETER 1716
(Epistle II – To the Right Honourable the Earl of Burlington)

O'er the green turf the miles slide away,
And Blandford ends the labours of the day.
The morning rose; the supper reckoning paid,
And our due fees discharg'd to man and maid,
The ready ostler near the stirrup stands,
And, as we mount, our halfpence load his hands.

Now the steep hill fair Dorchester o'erlooks.
Border'd by meads, and wash'd by silver brooks.
Here sleep my two companions eyes supprest,
And, propt in elbow-chairs, they snoring rest:
I weary sit, and with my pencil trace
Their painful postures, and their eyeless face;
Then dedicate each glass to some fair name,
And on the sash the diamond scrawls my flame.
Now o'er true Roman way our horses sound.
Graevius would kneel, and kiss the sacred ground.
On either side low fertile valleys lie,
The distant prospects tire the travelling eye.
Through Bridport's stony lanes our route we take,
And the proud steep descend to Morcombe's lake.
As hearses pass'd, our landlord robb'd the pall,
And with the mournful 'scutcheon hung his hall.
On unadulterate wine we here regale,
And strip the lobster of his scarlet mail.

1720   *John Gay*

from
DORCHESTER AMPHITHEATRE

Who may misprize Dorchestrian hills? What though
They tower to no such height as looks with scorn
Over a dwindled plain; what though no crags
Be there to fortify; no forest belts
To gird them midway round; yet theirs, instead,
Are graceful slopes with shadowy dips between;
And theirs are breezy summits, not too high
To recognise familiar sights, and catch
Familiar sounds of life, the ploughman's call
Or tinkling from the fold. Yet thence the eye
Feeds on no stinted landscape, sky and earth
And the blue sea; and thence may winged thought,
Which ever loves the vantage point of hills,
Launch amid buoyant air, and soar at will.

1838   *John Kenyon*

8

HILL FORTS OF DORSET

Entrenched in sleep lies Eggardon,
That old bluff knight o' th' shire,
And at his feet, a crested son,
Tall Shipton, his esquire.
Meanwhile the Maiden in her fort –
Her sentry, Dorchester –
Dreams of the knight, their youthful court;
The watch for the foe, with her,
Were Fleet and Chesil-bank the prey.

"Come, knight, again bestride,
As once, the barrow, downland way;
Still claim me as your bride.
Lest Dorchester now make ado,
Bring sword and Shipton's spears,
And by the sea, should he pursue,
There's a camp-friend close, at Wears."

Awake, awake, proud Eggardon!
Maybe, our men forsook
The highland long ago; yet on
The air tall masts at Hooke
Send sparkling, instant messages;
Your duty may be theirs,
A radar-check on enemies,
As once were beacon flares.
Awake! Shake off the sea-fog, knight;
And let a cloud compose
A sunset mantle for the fight,
A Matterhorn of rose.

1955   George Montagu, Earl of Sandwich

DAYBREAK IN DORSET

It is not my fate that brought me here,
Though this is Hardy's land;
I am beyond my fate's frontier,
And in the realm of grace expand,
Heart truant and confused
With the flooding mystery –
A land so fertile, yet not alien tone.

Was not my language mere
Curt crumbling jargon of mauled rock,
Of purgatorial fire and sundering shock?
Yet the crabbed text grows pale
And I read instead the living litany
Of virgin earth unbruised
In winding tree-domed aisles of Blackmoor Vale.

Fate-ridden land, in Hardy's view,
Yet every mood I have glimpsed to-day,
On Dorset's face, each passionate hue,
Puts my bleak fate away.

I have seen the moment's fret
When thundery rain half vexed the little Stour,
And then the smile's full play
As clear sun poured on hills where the sheep fed
And through the thatch-warm villages I sped
Till summer stood serene,
Enfolding me in rich fulfilment, dower
Of Dorset's heart
My fancy long had set apart,
In dream-distilled Mappowder.

And I have seen
Fair golden evening drowse on Bulbarrow Hill
And on grey arch and parapet
Of old Sturminster bridge; then, all too soon,
Sherborne in twilight cloistered as the moon
In cool strong candour veered from Cranborne Chase.

And in each new discovery, each tumultuous thrill,
There was no place
For fear of shaping scourge, though Tess's frail
Sad ghost might haunt the mind.
I had left my fate behind:
There could be no betrayal
Save in the night of doubt; and stronger, louder
Than the slurred dubiety
Was the voice of faith's new day.

I am purged now
Even of my purgation: the furnace fires
Are hot in Cornwall, and cold is the sand,
But I take the gentler vow
To sun that ripens when the fierce flame tires.

I have shed the scabs of my hard destiny,
I have crossed the border, found the guiding hand,
And am made complete
In Dorset's tender touch, so magically sweet.

1950   *Jack Clemo*

THE RETURN OF THE NATIVE

Ah God! to see the pylons stride
Across the Dorset countryside!
To hear, so thunderous sweet and shrill,
The tank shells burst on Bindon Hill!

To smell the diesel fumes that wreath
The once chill air of Wareham Heath.
Lord! 'twould be very bliss to feel
Ringstead's last inch beneath the heel
Of Progress; paradise to know
Of Winfrith's radioactive flow,
And taste 'mid Lodmoor's rubbish tips
The ecstasy of fish and chips.
Stands there a yet unscheduled tree?
And is there money here for me?

1964   *H.M.G. Bond*

DORSET

John Fowles's book, The French Lieutenant's Woman:
"A grand ebullient portrait certainly"
Of Thomas Hardy's country, where however
I would not strike such sparkles. Slow and vocal
Amber of burring baritone
My Grandad's voice, not Hardy's, is what stays
Inside me as a slumbrous apogee,
Meridional altitude upon
Pastoral England's longest summer day.

O golden age! Bee-mouth, and honeyed singer!

1974   *Donald Davie*

NATURE RESERVE, DORSET

Keep out – except on business –
this is their land – the lizard and the roe-deer
find here a sanctuary
and the waterfowl returning
feel peace on the Little Sea.

So come with a microscopic eye
to watch the slow-worm and the adder crawl
unhindered in the sand,
but keep out every motor-tyre,
this is a tip-toe land.

1975   *Randle Manwaring*

CATTISTOCKY

(A Dorset fantasy, with apologies to all concerned, not least Lewis Carroll)

'Twas Swanage, and the Durdle Door
Did Swyre and Chettle in the Cerne;
More Crichel was the Gallows Gore,
And the Kimmeridge Pimperne.

"Beware the Cattistock, my son!
The jaws that bite, the paws that grub!
Beware the Lydlinch bird, and shun
The Batcombe Melbury Bubb."

He took his Poxwell sword in hand,
Long time his Motcombe foe he sought –
So rested he by the Todber tree,
And stood awhile in thought.

And as in Gussage thought he stood,
The Cattistock, with eyes of flame,
Came Bincombe through the Chalbury wood,
And Melplash as it Came!

One two! One two! And through and through,
The Poxwell blade went snicker-snack!
By Smacam Down and Puddletown,
He went Bockhampton back.

"And hast thou killed the Cattistock?
Come to my arms, my Dewlish boy!
O Hammoon day! Upcerne! Upwey!"
He Loders in his joy.

'Twas Swanage, and the Durdle Door,
Did Swyre and Chettle in the Cerne;
More Crichel was the Gallows Gore,
And the Kimmeridge Pimperne.

1978   *S. John Forrest*

LAND VIEWS

Where shall we sit us down to rest
To see the place you like the best?
Beneath that hollow oak's grey shell
We see the river-cloven dell,
Where pebble-broken waters flow
To dark bridge arches, bow by bow;
And you, as in your early days
You took your ways, went to and fro.

By yonder ash, above our track,
You see high Hambledon's blue back,
With rings cast up in olden time
Too steep, in hope, for foes to climb;
And there is Cromwell's Gap, where died
So many men of ours, who tried
To keep at bay, in deadly fight,
Old Cromwell's might, on that hill side.

On yonder knoll you have in sight
The broad-spread Duncliffe's lonesome height,
In upper winds, that sigh around
His wooded sides, with moansome sound;
The hill our elders, in the run
Of years on years, from sire to son,
Beheld from village homes beside
The Stour undried, one after one.

And on that right-hand hill, as falls
The sun, shine out high Shaston's walls,
That keep the height where stood of yore
The many tower'd Paladour,
Far up the floods of Stour,
Although full many houses cow'r
Below the hill, and there is seen
A churchyard green, above the tower.

1868   *William Barnes*

ABBEY WALK

Shaftesbury stands alone
ready for wind and hail,
up on a ridge, constantly braced
against the coldest gale.

The wind spins leaves at my feet
and sighs in the limes above;
huddled, I gaze from Abbey Walk,
absorbed in the view I so love.

The bleats of lambs new-born
and their anxious mothers' call
waft upwards from the fields below –
on the wind that finds us all.

Isn't it time for winter to end?
But the wind whines up Love Lane:
"Maybe it is, but maybe not yet...."
so Shaftesbury holds on again.

But daffodils speak up now,
their heads are beginning to show:
"Spring will come, and soon" they say
"not long now, you know!"

Old Shaston even more will become
a delight and a joy to know:
the hills, the stones,
the cobbled ways,
all will be singing, I know.

1980   *Ann Ford*

THE RIVER STOUR

Stour, of all our streams the dearest
Unto me, for thou wast nearest
    To my boyhood in my play,
Blest may be the sons and daughters
That beside thy wand'ring waters
    Have their hearth, and spend their day.
By happy homes of high and low
Flow on dark river, ever flow.

Thou through meady Blackmore wendest,
And around its hillslopes bendest,
    Under the cliffs, and down the dells;
On by uplands under tillage,
On beside the tower'd village,
    With its sweetly-chiming bells.
There go, dear stream, and ever flow
By souls in joy without a woe.

Wind around the woody ridges;
Shoot below thy archy bridges,
    Swelling by thy many brooks;
Gliding slowly in thy deepness;
Rolling fleetly at thy steepness;
    Whirling round the shady nooks;
And pass the lands that fall and rise
Below the sight of tearless eyes.

              ****

Glowing under day's warm sunning,
Sparkling with thy ripples' running,
    Taking to thee brooks and rills,
Valley-draining, dell-bewending,
Water-taking, water-sending,
    Down to dairy farms and mills,
O blest below each village tow'r
Be thy by-dwellers, gliding Stour.

1868   *William Barnes*

OVERLOOKING THE RIVER STOUR

The swallows flew in the curves of an eight
        Above the river-gleam
        In the wet June's last beam:
Like little crossbows animate
The swallows flew in the curves of an eight
        Above the river-gleam.

Planing up shavings of crystal spray
        A moor-hen darted out
        From the bank thereabout,
And through the stream-shine ripped his way;
Planing up shavings of crystal spray
        A moor-hen darted out.

Closed were the king-cups; and the mead
        Dripped in monotonous green
        Though the day's morning sheen
Had shown it golden and honeybee'd;
Closed were the king-cups; and the mead
        Dripped in monotonous green

And never I turned my head, alack,
        While these things met my gaze
        Through the pane's drop-drenched glaze,
To see the more behind my back....
O never I turned, but let, alack,
        These less things hold my gaze!

1917   *Thomas Hardy*

MARLOTT
(Marnhull)

Here is our village; her time lies
Softly beneath the Dorset skies
And morning breaks on hill and wood
That have for countless ages stood
Silent and still on either hand,
Green guardians of this quiet land.
And when the dusk on shadowed feet
Steals shyly up the village street,
Awake the gentle ghosts, no less,
Of Thomas Hardy, or of Tess,
And you may hear the spectral din
Of singing from the Pure Drop Inn.
Though passing years have changed the face
Of this once simple, rustic place,
Yet still in spring the apple bough
"Do lean down low" in Marlott now,
Where Tess's cottage snugly lies
Beneath the thatch, and summer skies
Are wide and bright as were her eyes.

1978   *Pamela Murray*

PLACE RHYME

If Duncliff wood be fair and clear,
You Stour boys need have no fear.
But if Duncliff wood doth wear its cap,
You Marnhull folk look out for that.

Anon

18

EDGEHILL INGHAM
Stalbridge

Romans were among those who freely chose
to live in this part of the upper Vale,
but today the calm town is that of those
given to finding items for resale.

The market-cross, over thirty feet high,
with its graven figures restored of late,
as ever is the place they meet to buy
fresh farm-produce, and to discuss their fate.

In very few places is this still done
But here it is a regular event.
For isolates – indeed for everyone –
it is a clan-gathering heaven-sent.

In the pale moonlight, when they have all gone,
what regard for Our Lord, his mother and St John?

1996   *Douglas Forward*

from
THE FAERIE QUEENE
Book IV, Canto XI

And there came Stoure with terrible aspect,
Bearing his sixe deformed heads on hye,
That doth his course through Blandford plains direct,
And washeth Wimborne meads in season drye.

1596   *Edmund Spenser*

19

MEMORIES OF ENGLAND
October 1940

I am glad, I think, my happy mother died
Before the German airplanes over the English countryside
Dropped bombs into the peaceful hamlets that we used to know –
Sturminster Newton, and the road that used to run
Past bridge, past cows in meadow,
Warm in sun,
Cool in the elm-tree's shadow,
To the thatched roofs of Shillingstone:

        ****

So gravely threatened now
That lovely village under the Barrow's brow,
Where peering from my window at dawn under the shelving thatch
With cold bare feet and neck scratched by the straw
I saw the hounds go by;
So gravely threatened the kind people there,
She in her neat front flower plot,
He like as not
Up in the 'lotment hoeing,
Or coming home to his supper of beer and cheese,
Bread and shallots.
These thoughts...
And thoughts like these....
Make me content that she, not I,
Went first, went without knowing.

1941   *Edna St Vincent Millay*

CHARAS CAME
Farnham

The general's neat white museum trim,
interests or amuses soldiers, past
a certain age; as it may explain him.
The range of exhibits displayed is vast.

The tight-lipped locals share the tribal dread
of innovation imposed by strangers;
This district saw his disturbing the dead
as exposing them to great dangers.

In time to come, their long anxious faces
may also have vanished, from this hard earth;
their skulls and crude tools, in the glass cases,
the basis for estimates of our worth.

1996   *Douglas Forward*

SALUTE TO THE BLANDFORD BY-PASS

All through the winter
The escarpment
Bore a white scar,
A curious wound
Across the bare chalk down.
Irrevocably the by-pass
Traversed its length,
And then in June
A sudden burst of scarlet
Flushed the banks on either side.
No Flanders Field could boast
A finer show
Of poppies, massed in strength.
No furrow ploughed
Could turn up such beauty
In its row.

1996   *Jean Marsden*

BELL RHYME

Knowlton bell is stole
And thrown into Whitemill hole;
All the devils in hell
Can't pull up Knowlton bell.

Anon

BADBURY RINGS

the sun goes down
and badbury turns

from sculpted balance
of light and dark
to brooding hump
the sky
in delicate pastels
fades slowly
mist and clouds
blue the horizon

in my eyrie
I watch time pass
alone
but sharing
another summer evening
with the countless ones
who have also sat and watched

the sun goes down
and badbury turns

1996   *Liz Reeve*

from
COPYING ARCHITECTURE IN AN OLD MINSTER
(Wimborne)

How smartly the quarters of the hour march by
That the jack-o'clock never forgets;
Ding-dong; and before I have traced a cusp's eye,
Or got the true twist of the ogee over,
A double ding-dong ricochetts.

Just so did he clang here before I came,
And so will he clang when I'm gone
Through the Minister's cavernous hollows – the same
Tale of house never more to be will he deliver
To the speechless midnight and dawn!

I grow to conceive it a call to ghosts,
Whose mould lies below and around,
Yes; the next "Come, come," draws them out from their posts,
And they gather, and one shade appears, and another,
As the eve-damps creep from the ground.

1917   *Thomas Hardy*

MINSTER BELLS

Burnished evening sunlight bathed warming fields
As blurs of feeding swallows scurried across an open sky
Instinct majestic in its swooping grace and flow.
A nervous deer froze suddenly
Hewn in granite caution
Whilst nearby bells pealed out their summer carol
And sonorous melody thrilled every silent copse.

Church call hovered like a stationary hawk
Echoing hesitantly past long-dead sculptured knights
And browsing ageing visitors
Whisperingly surprised in studied stained glass window gaze –
Armed only with their lightweight plastic cardigans
Fit for the palely illuminated crypt
And any relic of an idle moment.

The bells toll out like kindly thunder
And a distant pheasant struts with oriental ease
And defiantly shrieks an earnest summons to its mate.

1996   *C Korta*

CHRISTCHURCH
(On the Bridge)

A sound of bells, and waters whispering
Through pasture-meadows, marsh, and dunes of sand,
Lives in the name. Pleasant it is to stand
On the old bridge, and watch the weed-beds swing
I' the stream – the swallow dip its wing –
Just as ofttimes, when this was Abbey-land,
Maybe a Monk has stood, missal in hand,
What time the evening air, as now, did bring
                              The sound of bells.

Beautiful minster! you have had your day.
The message now hath struck another note.
The Spirit lasts, the Form must fall away.
The Godward thought, for ever and for aye,
Across the silence of the Ages floats –
                              Like sound of bells.

1900   *Clifford Harrison*

BOURNEMOUTH
(Branksome Chine)

Of Branksome Chine there lives to me and you
A pleasant picture: fir woods, dim and cool:
Lilies that whiten many a glassy pool:
A narrow gorge that opens into view
Sand-cliffs of amber and a sea of blue.
A place that's evergreen at heart of Yule!
The storm-wind seems its rage to tame and school,
Passing o'er sheltered nook and avenue
                              Of Branksome Chine.

The *Genius Loci* surely mourns in due
The day when first the Char-a-bancs it knew.
Earth's fairest scenes – says one – are as a rule
"Known but by few." One wishes that were true
(Granting that we ourselves select that few!)
                              Of Branksome Chine.

1900   *Clifford Harrison*

24

SEASIDE CITY

Busy traffic moves along a sunlit square,
  Sweet music from a bandstand echoes here and there,
Time for holidays –
  Along the zig-zag ways,
Of Bournemouth.

Stately pine-trees listen to the serenade,
  Down by a stream pink blossom lines a leafy glade,
Families have fun –
  Fascination has begun,
For Bournemouth.

Purple hills of Purbeck curve around the bay,
  White rocky Needles touch the sky above the spray,
Sea-gulls weave and play –
  Joy can ricochet,
In Bournemouth.

At evening golden ripples silhouette the strand,
  Young lovers dream together in their fairyland,
Won't need a crystal wand
  For magic moments found,
In Bournemouth.

1996   *Kay Ennals*

SIESTA TIME ON KIMBERLY ROAD
(Bournemouth)

Small grey trees with tired shoulders
Rustle out loud, as if alone,
The room-size shopfronts are all shut
Though noon, their centre-stages dark.
Gone are the street props and scenery:
The rainbow plastic buckets full of tights,
The rails of nearly-new, the bedding plants,
Tomato boxes and three wheeler bikes.
The awning flaps forlornly over Pilgrim's Produce
And there's not a car in sight.
No-one's cracking jokes in Kimberly News,
Or snapping up the bargains down in Snaps.
No-one's buying ties in the Guide Shop
Or sharpening mower-blades in Alan's Mower Shop,
And in the Dairy opposite the only sound
Is the drip-lop of the air conditioner,
The flies are scoring in the Salad Bowl,
The Post Office ink-pads are drying out
Where a cold half cup of tea is gathering fur.

Death sways deliberate from the Butcher's hooks
As the tilted axis of all the world is gathering
Where I stand, my grip gone, for on such a day
Men could land from Mars and go unnoticed down
Behind the backs of the fronts on slumbering
Kimberly Road.

1996   *Helen Flint*

STREET CRED

Spikey with rebellion,
Chained and studded,
She punks through Bournemouth's
Pastel-cottoned crowd.
ANARCHY her leather shouts,
But her baby girl,
Pink-suited, mob-capped,
In a bright new push-chair,
Pinkly laughs.

1996   *Malcolm Povey*

POOLE
from Devonshire Coast No 1 Sketchbook

Westward the sands by storms and drift have gained
A barrier, and that barrier maintained,
Backed by a sandy heath, whose deep-worn road
Deny'd the groaning wagon's ponderous load.
This branches southwards at the point of Thule,
Forms the harbour of the town of Poole.
A little headland on a marshy lake,
Which probably contemptuously was given
That deeps and shallows might for once be even.
The floating sea-weed to the eye appears,
And, by the waving medium seamen steers.
One straggling street here constitutes a town;
Across the gutter here ship-owners frown,
Jingling their money, – passengers deride,
The consequence of misconceived pride.

1811   *J.M.W. Turner*

PLACE RHYME

If Pool was a fishpool and the men of Pool fish,
There'd be a pool for the devil and fish for his dish.

Anon

27

BESIDE POOLE HARBOUR

Beside Poole Harbour I dream of boats

Out in the marsh
sensitive-eared sitka deer
feed on cord grass
Floating behind their squared rumps
Corfe Castle's broken-toothed stumps
Along an estuarine line of light
a black flickering of geese

From a moored queue
of sail-wrapped yachts
comes the clear water voice chatter
of small children
and the mast-clink
       clink clink
         of wind-rattled cables

On an island's sandy spit
sit drying cormorants
stuck side by side
like gothic spearheads

In vertical circles above
and over the mud sheen
goes the boastful gossip
of blackheaded terns
silenced by
like the sheet being folded
the downbeat
of an incoming heron's wings

Slow water walk
curlew stalk

I dream of boats

1975   *Sam Smith*

TARANTELLA
upon the closure of Millers' pork pie and butchery shop, Poole
High Street

Do you remember a car,
Miranda,
Do you remember that car
With wings and things
Made of sausage-strings,
Riding the skies on its cocktail pies,
With a chassis of veal, egg and ham?
And the cheerful persistence of counter assistants
(To the customer's every whim they pander)
Do you remember a car, Miranda,
Do you remember a car?
And the cheerful persistence of counter assistants
– The girl at the till
Would have been there still
But the Board closed the door with a slam.
Not the pat on the back
And the crack
Of the shopkeeping Mason's hand-shaking obeisance
To the wise
Enterprise
That raised him up in men's eyes,
And the Screech! Scrape! Din!
Of the moody old man with his violin
Cursing in
Every coin to the kerbside Oxo-tin.
Do you remember a car,
Miranda?
Do you remember a car?
Never more, Miranda,
Not now
The undertaker stands at the door
Measuring up as he sweeps you a bow.
Bells peal
As traders' names fade into shade.
As you sigh
At the Building Society's marble and steel
You feel
The old chill
Of the money-men making a kill.

1996   *Martin Blyth*

ARNE

I wish I could go to the sea to-day,
leave all my cares and walk away
down through the lane that leads to the shore
where the trees stand thick like a leafy door
that opens up to reveal the marshes
the grey mud flats and the tall reed grasses.
If you are a quiet nature-watcher
the cormorant and the oyster-catcher
will come so near
and seem to peer
at you,
as they start to groom their feathers sleek
on the water's edge of this silent creek.
Where the wooden ribs of a broken boat
protrude from the sand and will never float
or fish again far out to sea
but forgotten lie in this cemetery,
where the irises and sea-pinks grow
swaying to the salt winds blow.
If I could build a house just here
and watch those lovely things appear,
the plover with her little brood
searching constantly for food,
perhaps I would not wish to roam
if this were the place that I called home.

1996   *Ruth Kennedy*

BROWNSEA ISLAND

The boatman takes my elderly elbow
and spirits me across to the island
through the sea's surface glitter,
the deep water looking preoccupied
with far more important things.

Several presences inhabit the island;
noisiest are the exotic birds
shrieking the truth about colours,
with a hundred inward-looking eyes
they draw the sunlight into their tails.

Departed souls have neglected the daffodil-fields
and dig up no more clay for the old kilns:
their long-dead sepia faces stare at the camera,
the humps of their hovels are hidden
beneath a wilderness of rhododendrons.

More solid presences are the tall trees
but many suffered in the winter gales
and lie with their roots snaking the air:
we walk to the tips of their topmost twigs
and feel ourselves equal to the birds.

Now the boatmen are shouting for our pink tickets
so I stow this poem away for the mainland.
Little waves tell us what the sunlight is doing,
flickering like words on the surface of somewhere
where no words really exist.

1996   *Phillip Whitfield*

SUNDAY EVENING AT STUDLAND BAY

O'er countless hamlets simple bells have thrown
Their web of summons and are fallen still;
Cottage and hall in every shire are bowed
Submissive to God's will.

Ten thousand little village churches breathe
Their lowly offerings of praise and prayer,
Ascending to the infinitude of Heaven
Through England's evening air.

Here in this sheltered Dorset home is peace:
The gulls are folded from their soft-winged flight;
The sheep are penned; and all the earth is turned
Silently towards the night.

Only the sea makes murmur as it laves
The sandy bay and solemn, white cliff's base,
And, nearer heaven, over the moss-turfed down
The sweet wind roves its race.

The soul goes simply to its Maker here,
Up from this tiny house, in bygone days
By Norman fashioned for the self-same task
Of blended prayer and praise.

And so we stand in this enfolding hour,
England around us and the peace of heaven
Drawn down within our hearts, to our linked life
In promise greatly given.

Dear love, be this the beauty which shall wind
Eternally, and more and more, its peace
About our spirits, in this so-loved land,
Till our glad earth-days cease.

1922   *Lord Gorell*

LINES WRITTEN AT SWANAGE IN SEPTEMBER 1825

With sauntering step I musing stray
Along the marge of Swanage bay;
Her firm and sandy beach explore,
And hear the foamy billows roar
(While frequent sails attract the sight,
And beauteous Vecta's cliffs of white),
Or wander in the grove marine,
Where Pitt's presiding taste is seen,
In grotto and alcove display'd,
Beneath the elm's protecting shade;
Or listen to the wavy swell
Around the point of Peveril.
Sometimes my steps to Studland bend, –
Her heath-clad eminence ascend,
And view'd from thence in prospect clear,
Poole Bay, and Brownsea Isle appear;
And I have seen St Aldhelm's steep,
And Beacon Fane that skirts the deep,
The all-devouring deep, that gave
The Halsewell's crew a watery grave,
And though up th'heart-rending cry
Of Pierce's hapless family.
The near adjoining groves I hail,
That clothe the shops of Encombe vale,
Where, unembarrass'd by the cares
Of legal and of State affairs,
Time-honour'd Eldon rests awhile,
And tastes the sweets of Purbeck's Isle.

1825   *D. Cabanel*

DINOSAUR FOOTPRINTS UNEARTHED IN SWANAGE

Banana- or marmite-sandwiches by the sea,
And Charles and William in soppy grey-felt hats....
We tried our footprints out on the wet sand,
And Nanny unkindly called me Flatfootgee....

Commendable Swanage – remembered in soft pastel shades
Under light-blue or sailcloth skies – you had pearly shells,
And fresh air, and stones to climb over, and nursery decorum.
Later, there was a war and the sea was fenced off.

Once dinosaurs stamped thereabouts, picnicked, packed up;
Left antediluvian messages, a sort of *memento mori*
By way of their footprints. Ours are swept away,
And my first English days are March-coloured sea-borne wraiths.

1988   *Gerda Mayer*

ON DURLSTON HEAD, DORSET, SEPTEMBER

The climb rewarded, for a holm-oak grove
Rustled ahead at the road's end; and I,
Tracing a track that wildly interwove
Saw, in a flash of blue, the open sea.

London was now far from any skyline,
Tamarisk was fronding above – I turned,
Gazed across a sky of deepening wine
And back to the cool cliffs – and just discerned

The points of gulls skimming the crisp water,
Their dull peals tingeing the air with a last
Cadence of summer, balm like sun's wester,
Weightless as their shadows on top-spray cast.

1996   *Chris White*

CORFE CASTLE

Framed in a jagged window of grey stones
These wooded pastures have a dream-like air.
You thrill with disbelief
To see the cattle move in a green field.

Grey Purbeck houses by the sun deceived
Sleep with the easy conscience of the old;
The swathes are sweet on slopes new harvested;
Householders prune their gardens, count the slugs;
The beanrows flicker flowers red as flames.

Those to whom life is a picture card
Get their cheap thrill where here the centuries stand
A thrusting mass transfigured by the sun
Reeling above the streets and crowing farms.
The rooks and skylarks are OK for sound,
The toppling bastions innocent with stock.

Love grows impulsive here: the best forget;
The failures of the earth will try again.
She would go back to him if he but asked.

The tawny thrush is silent; when he sings
His silence is fulfilled. Who wants to talk
As trippers do? Yet, love,
Before we go be simple as this grass.
Lie rustling for this last time in my arms.
Quicken the dying island with your breath.

1945   *Alun Lewis*

A FLASH OF PURBECKS

A ring of above-roads, of a four-pronged beacon,
A flight of hills as seen from a room in the sky –
The hours continue to spin as though machines
Seeking masters, while taking us from nothing to nothing
Making a thin tape of life until we flag
And sink into our last beds, lost. The hills
Refuse to spin, refuse to coil cogs, to clatter;
Are secretive at night or in mist
Until, abruptly after a shower's fullness,
They shine, epiphanies above
Long miles of houses, above
What passed for skyline's Thule,
Urging you on beyond the houses.

Urging you to risk the climb in spring wind –
Blade-sharp on sea's cloud-edge in March,
And silver to the heart. The grey whaleback ridge
Floods green sudden as the gulls' flashes,
Taking the prospect westward to Corfe and Creech,
Crying to be walked.

1996   *Chris White*

CORFE CASTLE AT DUSK

the last angry red drains from the sky,
eyes closed, concentrating hard, I try to
tune in to violent thoughts travelling
down a thousand years and hope to feel
a shudder on the spot the martyr Edward died
(few stepmothers, even in fiction, were more
wicked than his) I shiver, but only because
a chill wind ripples my thin T-shirt – time
to quicken my pace, walk briskly away
half-stumbling, pursued by spooks; an owl hoots
but the desperate cries of the dying boy-king
will go unanswered tonight

1996   *Richard Green*

ENCOMBE

(from
A *dialogue between a poet and his servant*
In imitation of Horace, Book VII, Sat. VII)

S. From Encombe, John comes thundering at the door,
With, "Sir, my master begs you to come o'er,
To pass these tedious hours, these winter nights,
Not that he dreads invasions, rogues, or sprites."
Straight for your two best wigs you call,
This stiff in buckle, that not curl'd at all.
"And where, you rascal, are the spurs," you cry;
"And O! what blockhead laid the buskins by?"
On your batter'd mare you'll needs be gone,
(No matter whether on four legs or none)
Splash, plunge, or stumble, as you scour the heath;
All swear at Morden 'tis on life or death;
Wildly through Wareham streets you scamper on,
Raise all the dogs and voters in the town;
Then fly for six long dirty miles as bad,
That Corfe, and Kingston gentry think you mad.
And all this furious riding is to prove
Your high respect, it seems, and eager love:
And yet, that mighty honour to obtain,
Banks, Shaftesbury, Doddington, may send in vain.

1727   *Christopher Pitt*

Encombe was the seat of John Pitt, Esq.

WINTER AT KIMMERIDGE

searching footsteps,
velvet soft
through slatey shingle.
darkening cliffs,
strange, menacing,
deserted.
silent beauty,
pool of delight
on paynes grey water.
boulders
laced by seaspray
and seaweed.

1978   *Pamela Derry*

OLD DORSET WOMEN AND TANKS

In the waiting bus at Wareham
Sit a row of old village women,
Ready to drive into Corfe.
They are laden with baskets and bags.
Thundering by roar tanks,
Great inhuman, brutal weapons of war,
With gargoylish figures peering out of the turrets.
But the old women never turn their heads to look;
They nod and prattle together.

What matter these noisy tanks to them?
They who have been marketing?
Their interest is the business of living,
An old, old business.

Soon the bus moves on,
Moves to beneath the line of hills
Clear cut against the sinking sun.
They too are indifferent to warfare,
For many wars have passed beneath their heights.
They and the old women, belong to the eternal order of things.

1946   *Theodora Roscoe*

TYNEHAM

Thrown open to the public at week-ends,
the army ranges on the Purbeck coast
are paradoxically a place of peace.
We cheat a bit and sit a yard or two
beyond the "Danger cliff erosion" sign.
Invisible to walkers on the path,
protected from the curious in our "hide",
we share with gulls their view of rock-torn sea
four hundred feet below, where cormorants
use their long necks to fish the flooding tide.

The shore's arm curved towards its Portland fist,
cradling the blue-green sea of Weymouth Bay.
Six scolding gulls float up on thermal air,
their wings translucent when they cross the sun.
A croaking raven tumbles in display,
a hovering kestrel treads the morning breeze,
and buzzards mew among the valley oaks.
A sudden stir of general unease;
a peregrine is sighted high above.
He dives in "ton-up" stoop to grab a dove.

1996   *Edmund Harwood*

GULLS AT LULWORTH

there isn't much to choose down here
between the sea and the wind
(the gulls tying the two together)

or maybe the gulls are on about
the three hundred and sixty-six days
(this year) of christmas
and the way the light and the dark
are constantly in need of each other

the best fish (so the gulls say) don't
have to come in crinkly paper

1996   *R.G. Gregory*

THE GREEN VALLEY

Here in the green scooped valley I walk to and fro.
In all my journeyings I have not seen
A place so tranquil, so green;
And yet I think I have seen it long ago,
The grassy slopes, and the cart-track winding, so.

O now I remember it well, now all is plain,
Why twitched my memory like a dowser's rod
At waters hidden under sod.
When I was a child they told me of Charlemagne,
Of Gan the traitor, and Roland outmarched and slain.

Weeping for Roland then, I scooped in my spirit
A scant green Roncesvalles, a holy ground,
Which here in Dorset I've found:
But finding, I knew it not. The years disinherit
Their children. The horn is blown, but I do not hear it.

1925   *Sylvia Townsend Warner*

LLEWELYN POWYS ON CHALDON DOWN

The chilled fingers scatter
imaginary ice on the dark earth;
the sheep on the other side
of the single electrified wire
move nervously away from us,
as we follow the winding
rising and dipping chalk path
you must have walked so often.

The teeth have cropped short
the bleached grass, and from
the low round-shouldered
hillside comes the laughter
of hidden faces, echoed
by the cries of birds whose
blackness defies all thought
but treading on new snow.

Your unpainted summerhouse
still turns, hidden from sight
by your long vacated home,
as ever craning to see over
the stubbled ridge, to hear
the waves smashing fears
against the black white walls
of the tallest cliffs for miles.

If we take a large dose of death,
we can stand aside to let
you lead us along this narrowing
edge that skirts the dried poppies,
shadow you across the newly
turned soil, and join your search
for traces of those men whose lives
are found only in flaked grey stone.

1996   *R.G. Felton*

THE DOMES OF WINFRITH

The domes of Winfrith are a wondrous sight;
The mighty waves at Lulworth Cove hover
In awesome tremor. No need to fear the chains within
We'll duck and cover should the melt begin,
And grow lush barley with two-headed grain
Knowing two heads are better than one, the same
With us, who hope to God that we transmute in time
Before the heavy water goes on line.

The domes of Winfrith are a wondrous sight;
It is not sewage gushing through that pipe –
But a kind of seminal, a kind of time-clock
To be woven into fish and seaweed, to unleash
Brave new mutants on the South Coast folk.

1996   *Helen Flint*

PLACE RHYME

Wool streams and Combe Wells,
Fordington cuckolds stole Bindon bells.

Anon

41

T.E. LAWRENCE'S GRAVE AT MORETON

Rain clearing
Under the drooping cedar
Dead cones litter the graves of Lawrence
And Ethel Shrimpton, villager, died at 83.
In the church, at a distance,
Crowds um and ah
At the ice-sharp niceties of Whistler's windows
But for the raindrops
Here there is only silence.

I think of Lawrence in the desert
Under a burnished sun
In Bedouin clothes, riding a camel,
Leader of men
In the heady urgency of war.
Weaving his pattern of words
Round the pillars of wisdom

Or courting obscurity under a cloak of names.
A troubled spirit
Ever seeking escape.

Ethel I do not know.
Mother, cottager, farmer's wife.
One of Hardy's peasants perhaps.
Her family scattered
Casually round Lawrence.
Certain she rode no motorbikes or camels,
Camped in no deserts,
Hid under no false names.
Her deeds of simple heroism
Passed unnoticed from these quiet lanes.

Lawrence and Ethel share a common earth,
Side by side, bone by bone,
Man of destiny and woman of this place.
Yet when admirers come to pay respects
Ethel's gravestone is not left unread.

1991   *Neil Adams*

AD HENRICUM WOTTONEM
(Bere Regis)

Wotton, my little Bere dwells on a hill,
Under whose foot the silver trout doth swim,
The trout silver without and gold within,
Bibbing clear nectar, which doth aye distil
From Nulam's low head; there the birds are singing
And there the partial sun still gives occasion
To the sweet dew's eternal generation:
There is green joy and pleasure ever springing.
   O iron age of men, O time of rue,
   Shame ye not that all things are gold but you.

1598   *Thomas Bastard*

ATHELHAMPTON HALL

Scarred and strangely sad.
Yellow with age the outside stones
surround iron-laced windows
and time-encrusted doorways.
Shapes, curves and angles
blend to form a whole
that fits, like a hand in a glove,
the outside lands.
Inside these walls, oak panels cup the rooms
in sombre hands and everywhere
the furniture stands
beautiful, dead and still.

An ancient hall, where once
proud history passed and lived,
lies like some jewel
embedded in the hollows
where, in the dimness of the past,
England started many centuries ago.

1978   *Tony Stevenson*

PARADISE FOR SALE

(Dorset – 8 miles Dorchester In the valley of the River Piddle.
Kiddles Farm, Piddletrenthide. A Small Mixed Farm With Small
Period Farmhouse. Dining/Living Room, Kitchen,
3 Bed Rooms, Bathroom. – Adv. in *Country Life*)

Had I the shillings, pounds, and pence,
I'd pull up stakes and hie me hence;
I'd buy that small mixed farm in Dorset,
Which has an inglenook and faucet –
Kiddles Farm,
Piddletrenthide,
In the valley of the River Piddle.

I'd quit these vehement environs
Of diesel fumes and horns and sirens.
This manic, fulminating ruction
Of demolition and construction,
For Kiddles Farm,
Piddletrenthide,
In the valley of the River Piddle.

Yes, quit for quietude seraphic
Con Edison's embrangled traffic,
To sit reflecting on that skylark,
Which once was Shelley's, now is my lark,
At Kiddles Farm,
Piddletrenthide,
In the valley of the River Piddle.

I'm sure the gods could not but bless
The man who lives at that address,
And revenue agents would wash their hands
And cease to forward their demands
To Kiddles Farm,
Piddletrenthide,
In the valley of the River Piddle.
Oh, the fiddles I'd fiddle,
The riddles I'd riddle,
The skittles I'd scatter,
The winks I would tiddle!

Then hey diddle diddle!
I'll jump from the griddle
And live out my days
To the end from the middle
On Kiddles Farm,
Piddletrenthide,
In the valley of the River Piddle.

1962   *Ogden Nash*

CERNE GIANT

the quiet figure
fronts his hill
his space limited
by a puny fence
his right hand
grasps his club
in a gesture
that might be threatening

his clean chalk outline
carefully defined
by passing generations
although his cloak
and dog
lie hidden beneath the turf
now gently trodden
by grazing sheep

he maintains his erection
over the centuries
observing the seasons
while visitors from this other world
stand and gaze
expectantly

1996   *Joan Briggs*

THE MARTINS CHAPEL
(Puddletown)

The Martins now are gone,
Their long flight ended.
Into this nest of stone
The last is now descended.

All seasons through
They clung to their one dwelling,
War, peace and plague,
For years past hope of telling.

Now to a land they go
Beyond the farthest swallow.
God grant thy soul a wing
If thou shouldst wish to follow.

1958   *Clive Sansom*

THE MARTYRS DAY

The day has come, we pray for sun, Martyrs Day is here;
They gather here at Tolpuddle, they come from far and near,
They come to listen to those who know, and say how it should be
To remember those six brave men, who met beneath the tree.

So we rally to the flag, and raise our banners high;
We march the street, once again, to the sound of The Farmer's Boy.
There's people here from many trades, they come both man and wife;
Like six brave men, they only ask for a better deal in life.

1996   *E Chaffey*

CHARMINSTER

It's hard here: the lane at the gate
Pitted, harsh underfoot
Is an indication of place: another, wintry
Hedges sheared to brittle sticks.

It's hard here: across the lane
The cemetery's spindly fence rusts
Round crossed and modest stones:
Marks of tidied lives' remains

Coffined and trimmed, inscriptions
Delicately chiselled; a few names
Recently remembered, though most laid
In long-lost forgetfulness.

It's hard here: a cottage walls, once
Home, tell of cobbled centuries
Old as sorrow; of scarred hands
That hewed and hauled and built them here;

Of huddled lives, hidden or thrust
Forth to endure the perennial field;
Its roof as void as lives it sheltered,
Windows eyeless, door shut.

It's hard here: climb through the village
To hills older than sorrow, baring
Massive backs with immemorial
Indifference. See a red sun

Pale and melt into night pitted
With stars; frost on the lane, the gate;
A clenched fist close to the heart.

1996   *Frank Alcock*

DOMICILIUM
(Higher Bockhampton)

It faces west, and round the back and sides
High beeches, bending, hang a veil of boughs,
And sweep against the roof. Wild honeysucks
Climb on the walls, and seem to sprout a wish
(If we may fancy wish of trees and plants)
To overtop the apple-trees hard by.

Red roses, lilacs, variegated box
Are there in plenty, and such hardy flowers
As flourish best untrained. Adjoining these
Are herbs and esculents; and farther still
A field; then cottages with trees, and last
The distant hills and sky.

Behind, the scene is wilder. Heath and furze
Are everything that seems to grow and thrive
Upon the uneven ground. A stunted thorn
Stands here and there, indeed; and from a pit
An oak uprises, springing from a seed
Dropped by some bird a hundred years ago.

                    In days bygone –
Long gone – my father's mother, who is now
Blest with the blest, would take me out to walk.
At such a time I once inquired of her
How looked the spot when first she settled here.
The answer I remember. "Fifty years
Have passed since then, my child, and change has marked
The face of all things. Yonder garden-plots
And orchards were uncultivated slopes
O'ergrown with bramble bushes, furze and thorn:
That road a narrow path shut in by ferns,
Which, almost trees, obscured the passer-by.
Our house stood quite alone, and those tall firs
And beeches were not planted. Snakes and efts
Swarmed in the summer days, and nightly bats
Would fly about our bedrooms. Heathcroppers
Lived on the hills, and were our only friends;
So wild it was when first we settled here."

1916   *Thomas Hardy*

DOMICILIUM
"This for Remembrance"

Hereto we came, some thirty years ago
Herein we lived; your "Domicilium"
Was ours to cherish. Though we did not view
Your "voiceless ghost": here lovelier far, we knew
(Before the hastening years had swept away)
Much that remained unchanged since your far day.

We heard the starlings rustle in the thatch
Above our heads, and from the small trapdoor
Saw, tied to beams (still "rooftrees" at our time)
The dusten bundles of the earliest straw.

The small birds fluttered at their morning bath
In that high beechen pool, so close outside
The bedroom window, scattering sunkissed stars
While overflowing water stained the bole.

And when the moon was full and high above,
The frosted garden was a magic land
Where silver bushes stood amid the pools
Of their moon shades, as sun, in tropic lands.

Our first full moon rose red behind the pines
And we both ran to check if furze ablaze.
Till then we knew not that, in later day,s
Gazing out eastward from your Max Gate home
You saw it too, and in a verse you wrote
You'd thought it "fire on Heath-Plantation Hill".

In new laid snow beneath the windows here
We saw the footprints of the fallow deer
And traced their coming from the field of white
Between our curtains they'd "looked in" last night.

The glow-worms in the dark up on the Heath
We gathered on their leaves of grass and fern
To lay round garden sinks: their brilliant light
We thus could vision, greening through the night.

When on the Heath at time of frost or dew
We walked in moonlight, round each shade-thrown head
We each had haloes, seeing but our own
Just as in Tess you, of her comrades said.

Before our time the postman laid the mail
Out in the porch, or slipped below the door.
The letterbox you used so long forgot
Was cleaned, and opened up to use once more.

I read all this alone, as winter nighs.
The diary notes we wrote that we might share
Oft in our ageing lives those vanished joys;
But you are gone – there's no one on the stair.

1993   *Ruth Skilling*

AN INVITATION TO TEA
(William Bellows accompanies Edmund Gosse to Max Gate,
29 June 1927)

Setting off, sun shining,
new vistas ahead and the distant moorland
blue, we drew near at last
to "Casterbridge"; asked the way
to Max Gate.....

Turning into a gravel drive,
found the house hidden among bushes.

So this was Hardy at eighty-eight!
Figure erect, hair silvered,
a lined face but the voice youthful.
Welcome waited at table;
there were raspberries – what raspberries!

And such talk! Gosse leading,
myself the stranger offering
a modest, occasional word.
We spoke of D'Urberville tombs
recently seen, the battered stonework.

Vandals, said Hardy: and then all
settled down to story-telling.

No tired author this. Voice well-sustained,
eyes twinkling, a man sprightly
in mind and act. Skipping upstairs
he brought down books,
Tess translated into fine French.

We asked a photograph.
And was our host still writing?
His wife assured us..... Time then to go.
Sun on the road; all still on "Egdon Heath".
A day to savour, remember.

1984   *M.A.B. Jones*

BARNES AND HARDY

We pass them daily, the two houses,
driving into Dorchester. The first, wide open,
oldy-worldy with thatched roof and lawns,
the rectory where the poet-parson lived
and died, and saw his wife die,
and from which in quaint knee-breeches,
with palmer's staff, he made his visits
until the day he made his last one,
to Came Church, the light glinting
on his coffin, to give that curious signal
to his young friend then setting out.

For all his confidence he must have had
his doubts, with Darwin battering on
his library door, but his faith,
an ark well made to stand the floods,
floated weather-cock high above the tumult.
The poems now abandoned, he wrote
in spiked and painful hand sermons
to comfort Dorset countrymen.

Ascending the hill we pass the second house,
where the shrubberies close in and a forbidding
sign chokes off enquirers. Here his ghost
– and how obsessive were his ghosts –
might smile today at the no-entry notice,
might smile in retrospect at bonfires,
cover-ups, biographies. Here he stood
that day, and whatever signal his innocent
old friend sent across dusty road
and open field, his own signal's flash is clear.
His tell-tale heart, encasketed,
shouts to us from the walls of every line
across the intervening years
as we pass the houses, pass our lives.

There is no comfort for us in the songs
except in the grace of their singing,
no resolution to our tales
but in the truth of their telling.

1978   *Michael Biddulph*

THE LAST SIGNAL
11 October 1886 – A Memory of William Barnes
(Winterbourne Came)

Silently I footed by an uphill road
That led from my abode to a spot yew-boughed;
Yellowly the sun sloped low down to westward,
And dark was the east with cloud.

Then, amid the shadow of that livid sad east,
Where the light was least, and a gate stood wide,
Something flashed like fire of the sun that was facing it,
Like a brief blaze on that side.

Looking hard and harder I knew what it meant –
The sudden shine sent from the livid east scene;
It meant the west mirrored by the coffin of my friend there,
Turning the road from his green.

To take his last journey forth – he who in his prime
Trudged so many a time from that gate athwart the land!
Thus a farewell to me he signalled on his graveway,
As with a wave of his hand.

1917   *Thomas Hardy*

REQUIEM FOR DORCHESTER WEST

Built by Brunel in the glorious age
Of Victorian power and the great broad gauge,
Rusted it stands with leprous wall
Daubed with graffiti, but still recalls
The grandeur that was steam.
Now the vandals have done their worst:
Wires ripped out and pipes are burst.
Even the hut that was built in place
Of the roof that spanned the rails with grace
Was set on fire and sprayed blue
And serves the drunks as a public loo.
Ghost of Isambard, do not despair,
Your masterpiece still stands four-square,
So sturdily built that it won't fall down,
A shabby reminder to the town
That one day soon it may afford
To see its former face restored.

1989   *Kenneth Leigh*

from
DORCHESTER AMPHITHEATRE
(Maiden Castle)

Fair, amid these, art thou, camp-crested Mount,
In some far time, for some forgotten cause,
Named of the Maiden. Nor doth surer lore
Attest if Briton or if Roman wound
Those triple trenches round thee; regular
As terraces, by architect up-built
For princely pleasure-ground, or those, far-famed,
By ancient hunters made – so some have deemed –
Or else by Nature's self in wild Glenroy.
Along thy sides they stretch, ring above ring,
Marking thee from afar....who so stays,
And climbs the turf-way to thy tabled top,
Shall reap a fuller wonder; shall behold
Thy girdled area, of itself a plain,
Where widely feeds the scattered flock; shall mark
Thy trenches, complicate with warlike art,
And deep almost as natural ravine
Cut in the mountain; or some startling rent
In the blue-gleaming glacier; or as clefts,
Severing the black and jagged lava-walls,
Which old Vesuvius round his crater flings,
Outworks, to guard the mysteries within.
But these are smooth and verdant. Tamed long since,
Breastwork abrupt and pallisaded mound
Are, now, but sloping greensward.

1838   *John Kenyon*

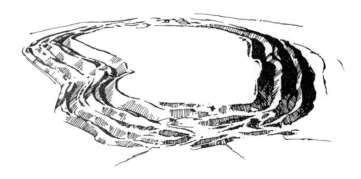

54

A SHEEP FAIR
(Poundbury Hill)

The day arrives of the autumn fair
    And torrents fall,
Though sheep in throngs are gathered there,
    Ten thousand all,
Sodden, with hurdles round them reared:
And, lot by lot, the pens are cleared,
And the auctioneer wrings out his beard,
And wipes his book, bedrenched and smeared,
And rakes the rain from his face with the edge of his hand,
    As torrents fall.

The wool of the ewes is like a sponge
    With the daylong rain:
Jammed tight, to turn, or lie, or lunge,
    They strive in vain.
Their horns are soft as finger-nails,
Their shepherds reek against the rails,
The tied dogs soak with tucked-in tails,
The buyers' hat-brims fill like pails,
Which spill small cascades when they shift their stand
    In the daylong rain.

Postscript

Time has trailed lengthily since met
    At Pummery Fair
Those panting thousands in their wet
    And woolly wear:
And every flock long since has bled,
And all the dripping buyers have sped,
And the hoarse auctioneer is dead,
Who "Going – going!" so often said,
As he consigned to doom each meek, mewed band
    At Pummery Fair.

1925　　　　　　　　　　　　　　　*Thomas Hardy*

PLANNING AHEAD

I will live in Martinstown
And keep a pair of Jacob sheep,
I'll spin their wool to wind me round,
Their hollow bells shall soothe my sleep.

And they shall crop the Dorset grass
And thicker, browner grow their fleece;
The days shall pass, the nights shall pass,
And my contentment shall increase.

The churchyard clock shall strike the hours,
The days and weeks and months shall pass;
My flock shall crop among the flowers
That patchwork all the Dorset grass.

The summer sun shall warm us through,
And if the snow in winter fall
Our coats of brown will be new,
It will not worry us at all.

I'll live my life without a frown
And sleep a warm and dreamless sleep,
When I can live in Martinstown,
And keep a pair of Jacob sheep.

1978   *Kay Hargreaves*

from
THE ROYAL TOUR

He reaches Weymouth – treads the Esplanade –
Hark, hark, the jangling bells! the cannonade!
Drums beat, the hurdigurdies grind the air;
Dogs, cats, old women, all upon the stare:
All Weymouth gapes with wonder – hark! huzzas!
The roaring welcome of a thousand jaws!

*****

The Mail arrives! hark! hark! the cheerful horn,
To Majesty announcing oil and corn;
Turnips and cabbages, and soap and candles;
And lo, each article Great Caesar handles!
Bread, cheese, salt, catchup, vinegar, and mustard,
Small beer, and bacon, apple-pye and custard:

All, all from Windsor greets his frugal Grace,
For Weymouth is a d-mn'd expensive place.

*****

And now to Delamot's the Monarch speeds:
He catches up a score of books, and reads –
Learns nothing – sudden quits the book abode –
Orders his horse, and scours the Dorset road.
He's in again! he boards the barge – sets sail –
Jokes with sailors, and enjoys the gale:
Descants on winds and waves – the land regains,
And gives the Tars just nothing for their pains!

1796   *John Wolcot*

ON THE ESPLANADE
Midsummer: 10 pm

The broad bald moon edged up where the sea was wide,
Mild, mellow-faced,
Beneath, a tumbling twinkle of shines, like dyed,
A trackway traced
To the shore, as of petals fallen from a rose to waste,
In its overblow,
And fluttering afloat on inward heaves of the tide:-
All this, so plain; yet the rest I did not know.

The horizon gets lost in a mist new-wrought by the night:
The lamps of the Bay
That reach from behind me round to the left and right
On the sea-wall way
For a constant mile of curve, make a long display
As a pearl-strung row,
Under which in the waves they bore their gimlets of light:-
All this was plain; but there was a thing not so.

Inside a window, open, with undrawn blind,
There plays and sings
A lady unseen a melody undefined:
And where the moon flings
In shimmer a vessel crosses, whereon to the strings
Plucked sweetly and low
Of a harp, they dance. Yea, such did I mark. That, behind,
My Fate's masked face crept near me I did not know!

1925   *Thomas Hardy*

THE MIGUEL D'AQUENDA; WEYMOUTH

The shepherd Britons, dwellers by the sea,
Who watched the dark Phoenicians hither come,
Or later heard, along the banks of Frome,
The Roman eagles scream, and turned to flee
To that green rampart on the Dorset lea,
Were not more troubled for their gods and home
Than when our fathers saw above the foam
The great D'Aquenda's galleon going free.
Men clenched their fist and muttered; women pale,
Pale as the Lulworth cliffs, went sobbing by:
"And is all lost, and are we prize to Spain?
And have our Weymouth gallants fought in vain?"
When out above the huge D'Aquenda's sail
They saw old England's glorious ensign fly.

1887   *H.D. Rawnsley*

SEALINK (WEYMOUTH)

every morning
about seven o'clock
the ship comes
across the channel
straight out of the sea
into our window

but not quite
when it turns
south-westward into harbour
we feel denied
the smell of continental cooking
so much news
of the world that fails
to reach our ears

at the same time
in another room
I am waiting waiting
for you too
to come up out of the sea

1996   *R.G. Gregory*

PORTLAND VIEWS

wherever there's a tear in the fabric
around weymouth – portland appears

from abbotsbury hill it's just a long
thin line humped at one end

closer (from chesil beach) a head-on
massive lump of rock gnashed by the sea

if you stand at sandfoot castle
there's a military feel – an armed guard

of an island harsh with prisons
snarling with secrets visitors don't probe

but on the road up out of town
towards the east a different spirit

rides inland over caravans and hedges
especially in soft light

portland softens like a pear
in syrup (yearning to be consumed)

elsewhere at other times it broods
a sleeping lion its paw upon

the carcase of its prey – but look
at portland if you can by night

its outline traced by street lights
its harshnesses seduced to

shadows – then the island hangs
beneath the sky in still festivity

its truths intact its wounds of stone
find blessing in the herbal dark

nothing of this of course is meaningful
unless inside us all there rests

a portland ravaged daily ill-at-ease
that has to use the night-time

for its solace – and each glimpse we get
of it assuages different guilts

1996   *R.G. Gregory*

PLANET PORTLAND

Iceland was less strange
                in its cinder deserts,
Lapland in drizzling twilight
                was less desolate
than this suburban moonland,

this worn old tooth
                attached by one thin strand
to the reassuring
                English face of Weymouth.
Sundays have scuffed its Pulpit.
                Shacks of cafes
steam "Teas" and swell with doughcakes.

Bony in flowering South,
                its main crop stone,
no proper island
                but an overnight
St Kilda at some tides,
                that land's-arm keeps
a freak sea up its sleeve,

harbours spare gales,
                when the whole boat is pushed,
an old tug unaccustomed
                to deep oceans,
on to the high waves' contours.

All burrows, moon-holed,
                carious with caverns.
Grained in its part-time islanders
                this superstition:
never, whatever you do,
                mention those puff-tailed
hopping mammals
                just in case you end up,
your frayed rope
                to the mainland severed,
put out to sea for ever.

1995   *Elsa Corbluth*

CHESIL WORDS

They are round, rubbed by time and motion
ceaselessly whispering, touching as parting
listing, murmuring to and fro.

Chesil words form beaches of wisdom,
discussing all day and all night
the sea, its dawn and its end.

Sometimes they bubble
sighting forward and back
asking forgiveness by swaying.

Sometimes they foam
gnash stony teeth
as they toss their message:

"Strange atoms in this sea were born
bundled and shaped like crown of thorn
twisted and meshed by word from the deep
until up the beach, as life, could creep.
Leaving the sea, soon leaving the land
living matter shall weave a band
across starlit heavens to where space must bend
and all words from all deeps into angels blend."

1996   *John Spencer*

THE QUARRYMAN

Under the sky he works all day,
Tanned by the sun's bright golden ray,
Battered and bruised by wind and rain,
Slogging and striving the stone to gain.
Tough, strong and rangy in stature growing,
Beaded by sweat and body a-glowing,
Raiming and swinging the tools of his trade,
Twibell and kivel, pickaxe and spade.
Blowing and chipping, cutting and shaping,
With muscles strained taut and aching,
And then to hang the iron chains
Around the stone with quiet disdain,
To load and send to other lands
Erect and gleaming in the sands –
To watch o'er friend and foe for ever.

1996   *Bob Wollage*

ABBOTSBURY GARLAND DAY

Flowers from the meadow, flowers from the lane,
Flowers from the meadows we gather again.
Flowers from the gardens so bright and so gay,
For it's Garland Day, down Abbotsbury way.

Patter of small feet a-down the lane,
Echoes of laughter resounding again.
Children's sweet voices so gay,
For it's Garland Day, down Abbotsbury way.

All through the village tripping so gay,
Showing their garlands all the spring day,
Then waiting the Blessing that grave voices say,
For it's Garland Day, down Abbotsbury way.

Travelling onward toward the beach,
Down to the Fleet's calm by Chesil's long reach,
Bearing their garlands all the long way,
For it's Garland Day, down Abbotsbury way.

There, where slight waves break, fishermen wait,
To take the garlands, now the day's late.
Gently the full tide bears them away,
Garland Day's ended, down Abbotsbury way.

1961   *Olive M Philpott*

ST CATHERINE'S HILL CHAPEL, ABBOTSBURY

A prayermark, nothing taller between
hilltop and heaven,
buttressed against salt winds it faces
sunrise, firm of purpose,
exemplar of heroic loneliness
like Catherine and the spinsters whom she blesses.

It could have pushed out of the hill's bones
before men needed saints to live by,
the dried piscina, empty pedestals
seeming now mere outcrops of stone.

It has seen faiths and fashions pass,
the abbey dismantled, the small fields razed.
Its spirit, stubborn over the wheeling world,
rides the centuries unbroken.

1996   *A C Clarke*

MONUMENT AT BLACK DOWN TO
ADMIRAL SIR THOMAS MASTERMAN HARDY

High on Black Down
I touch the stone column that rises skyward
like a land-locked lighthouse

surrounded as it is, below and beyond
by an undulating ocean of Wessex hills
stretching to a far sparkle of restless sea.

I see the boy from Portesham here beside me
gazing at distant ships square rigged in full sail
become a tall man wearing cocked hat and uniform

as captain of Nelson's famous flagship, Victory.
To Channel mariners, his Dorset memorial
stands as a landmark, a true waypoint, compass guiding.

Sailors value this man of the sea.
His constant mark on the chart of their lives.

1996   *Peneli*

WEST BEXINGTON ON SEA

Perhaps there is a part of me,
Still at West Bexington on Sea.

Where the land slopes to the ocean.
Where the Lyme Bay breakers crash
In perpetual emotion;
Wave by wave my hopes are dashed.

I know there is a part of me,
Still at West Bexington on Sea.

Where the wild gulls of Devon
Circle wild in mocking wheels,
Diving through the edge of heaven;
Now I know how hell can feel.

And yet there is a part of me,
Still at West Bexington on Sea.

Where the furious force-eight tears
And rips at rocks and leaning trees.
I hear her in the battered air
And something in my heart agrees;

There'll always be a part of me,
Here at West Bexington on Sea.

1988   *Mike Read*

PROPHECY FOR WEST DORSET

Woe to you! Woe!
Bridport and Beaminster
Charmouth and Chideock
Said the prophet.

For your old men have dreamed dreams
When they should have been awake,
And your young men have seen visions
Through a haze of hashish.
And your women have talked
And talked and gossiped and
Held coffee mornings and tea parties
Till there is not a donkey
With a pair of hind legs
Between here and Hindhead
Said the prophet.

You have abandoned the things that matter
For love of the things that do not matter,
And this shall be your punishment:
To become more and more obsessed
With less and less important things
Until you are utterly absorbed
By the totally meaningless
In an agony of anti-climax
Said the prophet.

Your highways shall be clogged with cars
As your hearts are clogged with avarice,
And the price of everything shall go up
Until chips are as rare as chastity,
And there shall be no more trains
Said the prophet.

Seven plagues shall come upon you:
Housing shortage and health hazards,
Parking meters and public lavatories,
And the three dreadful horsemen
Politics, publicity and population,
And still you will harden your hearts
Said the prophet.

Your seas will run with sewage
And you will not repent.
A penny will go on the price of beer
And you will not repent.
Bingo will be banned
And still you will not repent.
So you will come
Finally and inexorably
To the great and terrible day
Of the Last Jumble Sale.
Then shall the sheets be separated from the costs.
Nothing shall be overlooked.
For Lo!
Every hair that your neighbour's cat
Has left on your sitting-room sofa
Has been numbered,
Said the prophet.

Woe to you Bridport on that day.
Your town hall shall be replaced
By a multi-storey car park.
Woe to you Beaminster.
Your pseudonym shall be expunged for ever
From the novels of Thomas Hardy.
Woe to you Chideock and Charmouth.
For you shall never be bypassed,
Said the prophet.

And your names shall pass into history
As no more than sordid suburbs
Of the Greater West Dorset urban sprawl...
But if there shall be found in your midst
Even one man or woman
Who cares more about what people are
Than where they live,
All shall be spared
Just for the fun of it
Said the prophet.

1978   *"Jeremiah"*

from
POLY-OLBION
(Bridport)

And Car, that comming downe unto the troubled Deepe,
Brings on the neighbouring Bert, whose batning mellowed banke,
From all the British soyles, for Hempe most hugely ranke
Doth beare away the best; to Bert-port which hath gain'd
That praise from every place, and worthilie obtain'd
Our cordage from her store, and cables should be made,
Of any in that kind most fit for Marine trade.

1612   *Michael Drayton*

BRIDPORT HARBOUR

Hill-warded haven, creek well found
To sailors on thy stormy shore,
When 'midst the waters' deaf'ning roar,
They step on this thy peaceful ground,
As blest with happy homes, at hand,
Or strangers on a foreign land.

As softly sinks from fear to rest
The hunted stag, at last, hound free,
The ship that ploughs the stormy sea
Here stills her billow-beaten breast,
And yields her welcome freight to fill
Her hold with works of Bridport skill.

Here, fair from ev'ry shipwright's tool,
The new ship plunges from the stocks,
And chafes her first white foam, and rocks
On heaving waters of thy pool,
Now soon to waft her crew, in hope,
O'er longsome tracts of sea-wide scope.

The birds, where lay Prometheus bound,
Still ate, with everlasting bills,
His growing lungs, and these two hills
So yield to eating waves their ground,
That wastes in this receding shore,
But wastes, alas! to grow no more.

How many untold years have run
Since those two now half hills were whole,
And man beheld the waters roll
Where they sank, grassy to the sun,
Long ere the sea had cast the sand
And far-borne pebbles on this strand.

May ev'ry ship that commerce sends
From thee, O peaceful little creek,
Come back full-rigged, without a leak,
With men to wives, and friends to friends;
May Heaven speed both to and fro
All ships that here may come and go.

1872   *William Barnes*

GOLDEN CAP
(Visitors to this beautiful spot on the coast may have seen the simple stone
which prompted the following)

She climbed at dusk to the cliff-top,
his casket clasped to her breast, and
witnessed only by stars and the sea,
she scattered his ashes on the wind.
Silently she set a stone, boldly and
simply inscribed, that in this spot
he held so dear, her daffodils would
rise each year, to dance between the
stars and the sea,
                    for him alone –
                         her son.

1996   *Robert Lumsden*

LINES ON LYME REGIS

Lyme, although a little place,
I think it wondrous pretty;
If 'tis my fate to wear the crown,
I'll make of it a city.

1685   James, Duke of Monmouth (attrib.)

LYME REGIS

Brine-razored stone and weather-cleansed walls
Its houses all shapes and individual,
Lyme Regis hunched where Dorset hills
Come to the sea. A resort for the annual

Visitor to merge his character in sand
And sea; to sneak a look at
Girls and postcard-smut; to land
Mackerel aboard a hired boat out

In the wide wave-silvered bay where
Fated Monmouth once sailed
To land a ragged army there
And begin the sad invasion that failed.

An iodine miasma rises from the harbour
Where clumps of seaweed dry.
Fish and crabs decay after the heavy labour
When the tide runs high.

And brown-faced men deftly handle the fish
Humping along the grey stone wall
Baskets: each heaped with luminous fish.
Stranded boats lie in mud, their tall

Masts a forest of spears. And the harbour's clutter
Is somehow symbolic of such a town
"In Season" – with its shell shops, its clatter
And its visitors moving up and down.

1970   *William Oxley*

ON THE COBB AT LYME REGIS

Here no one wins because no one contends.
The white wall curves, wheels, skating out to France,
And I walk on it, between warm water
And cold, little boats and leviathans.

Dangerous the sea is; for all I know
It is even now, underneath the skin,
Battering the sea-wall with drowned sailors
Or countrymen who carelessly fell in.

But there is no Poseidon any more
To rise with a seventh wave and thunder,
To turn on all taps and overwhelm me
Gone suddenly shapeless like a spider.

If I had magic to keep the sea down
I would feel exceedingly complacent
And walk the wall like Nelson at Port-Royal
Conscious of skill to blunt any trident.

But this safety is different. I know
From my teachers what is impossible.
I am in no danger, the sea cannot rise,
Which is the most frightening thing of all.

1967   *Patricia Beer*

from
A DORSET IDYL
September 1878
(Holcombe near Lyme)

Dear land, where new is one with old:
Land of green hillside and of plain,
Gray tower and grange and tree-fringed lane,
Red crag and silver streamlet sweet,
Wild wood and ruin bold,
And this repose of beauty at my feet:-

Fair Vale, for summer day-dreams high,
For reverie in solitude
Fashion'd in Nature's finest mood;
Or, sweeter yet, for fond excess
Of glee, and vivid cry,
Whilst happy children find more happiness

Ranging the brambled hollows free
For purple feast; – till, light as Hope,
The little footsteps scale the slope;
And from the highest height we view
Our island-girdling sea
Bar the green valley with a wall of blue.

1881   *Francis Turner Palgrave*

A SONG FOR LODERS

When frost lies thick on Eggardon,
And every pool begins to freeze
From Muckleford to Nettlecombe,
And hills are hung with sparkling trees,
O, then, to Loders we must go
Before the world is drowned in snow.

> So here, my dear, and there, my dear,
> The air is singing Love tonight,
> And you, my dear, and you, my dear,
> Are trudging home in winter light.

When mists fall low on Eggardon,
And morning reddens sea and sky,
From Vinney Cross to Powerstock
The flocks of silent starlings fly,
O, then, as evening breathes farewell,
We take the rutted road to Bell.

> So, up, my dear, and down, my dear,
> The house is bringing Love tonight,
> And you, my dear, and you, my dear,
> Are trudging home in winter white.

When stars shine clear on Eggardon,
And field and fold are hushed with sleep,
From Yondover to Askerswell
The lanterns burn for wandering sheep,
O, then, for us those lanterns burn,
And, one by one, we shall return.

> So, swing, my dear, and chime, my dear,
> The tower is ringing Love tonight,
> And you, my dear, and you, my dear,
> Are trudging home in winter bright.

1972   *Leonard Clark*

A PREHISTORIC CAMP

It was the time of year
Pale lambs leap with thick leggings on
Over small hills that are not there,
That I climbed Eggardon.

The hedgerows still were bare,
None ever knew so late a year;
Birds built their nests in the open air,
Love conquering their fear.

But there on the hill-crest,
Where only larks or stars look down,
Earthworks exposed a vaster nest,
Its race of men long flown.

1939   *Andrew Young*

from
THE CHIMES OF CATTISTOCK

Into the Vale of Dorset flock the people;
Old men and young, maids, wives, and children flock
For half a mile all round about the steeple,
To listen to the Chimes of Cattistock.
    O happy Bells,
    Your music peals and swells
    Through the clear air
    In the green valley there!
    How many listen
    To your bright music, risen
    On farm and meadow,
    On homes in sun and shadow,
    On wildwood bowers,
    And blooming garden-flowers!
    O brave Bells swinging!
    O waves of happy ringing!
In the green western valley sing your flock
To joy again, sweet Chimes of Cattistock!

1929   *Eleanor Farjeon*

BE'MI'STER

Sweet Be'mi'ster, that bist a-bound
By green an' woody hills all round,
Wi' hedges, reachen up between
A thousan' vields o' zummer green,
Where elems' lofty heads to drow
Their sheades vor hay-meakers below,
An' wild hedge-flow'rs do charm the souls
O' maidens in their evenen strolls.

When I o' Zunday nights wi' Jeane
Do saunter drough a vield or leane,
Where elder-blossoms be a-spread
Above the eltrot's milk-white head,
An' flow'rs o' blackberries do blow
Upon the brembles, white an snow,
To be outdone avore my zight
By Jean's gay frock o' dazzlen white:

Oh! then there's nothen that's 'ithout
Thy hills that I do ho about, –
Noo bigger pleace, noo gayer town,
Beyond thy sweet bells' dyen soun',
As they do ring, or strike the hour.
At evenen vrom thy wold red tow'r.
No: shelter still my head, an' keep
My bwones when I do vall asleep!

1844   *William Barnes*

BROADWINDSOR AND BURSTOCK CHARGE BOOK, 1846-48

Masterman Hardy's Monument
was still arising when
William Moran, the Constable,
took up his book and pen,
listed the village vagabonds
and catalogued the crime
in a firm hand, which said: *I am
the conscience of my time.*
To Justices at Beaminster
he brought each prize in season.
The poachers, drunkards, turnip thieves
seemed a sufficient reason
why few had sheets, and many, straw.
Moran's book showed it best
to keep the poor at arm's length, in
the Rural Interest.
Now all their doings are as dust
along the village street;
the hireling's hovel, a retired
Rear Admiral's retreat.
The old and vulnerable complain:
"Our policing's done by van.
We've lost our old communities."
True. *But we've lost Moran.*

1996   *Martin Blyth*

UNDER HIGH-STOY HILL

Four climbed High-Stoy from Ivelwards,
Where hedge meets hedge, and cart-ruts wind,
Chattering like birds,
And knowing not what lay behind.

We laughed beneath the moonlight blink,
Said supper would be to our mind,
And did not think
Of Time, and what might lie behind...

The moon still meets that tree-tipped height,
The road – as then – still trails inclined;
But since that night
We have well learnt what lay behind!

For all of the four then climbing here
But one are ghosts, and he brow-lined;
With him they fare,
Yet speak not of what lies behind.

1925   *Thomas Hardy*

from
LEWESDON HILL

Up to thy summit, Lewesdon, to the brow
Of yon proud rising, where the lonely thorn
Bends from the rude South-east, with top cut sheer
By his keen breath, along the narrow track
By which the scanty-pastured sheep ascend
Up to the furze-clad summit, let me climb;
My morning exercise; and thence look around
Upon the variegated scene, of hills,
And woods, and fruitful vales and villages
Half-hid in tufted orchards, and the sea
Boundless, and studded thick with many a sail.

1788   *William Crowe*

SHERBORNE FROM THE SLOPES

A clear pale sky; and in the silver West
A white sun sinking low, lighting the land
With radiance ere he leaves her to her rest;
And crosswise o'er the prospect, gentle fann'd
By the chill springtide wind, a haze doth stand
White like the sunlight, thin, and not opprest
With heavier fumes; but showing the long crest
Of blue hills in the distance gloomily grand.

Above, a slope with unleafed branches laced;
Below, the gleam upon the rail where glides
A slowing train by Yeo's reflecting tides;
Beyond, the smoke-veiled town where, boldly placed,
With the departing sun's last glory graced,
The lordly Abbey on the housetops rides.

written 1910   *Giles Dixey*

APOLOGY IN ANGLO-SAXON ALLITERATIVE METRE

Over eleven hundred years ago,
The kings of Wessex warred against the Danes;
Within a decade two of them were dead, and here
In Sherborne lie, their crowns laid down;
Their youngest sibling grasped the sceptre firm;
By sword and craft at sea and on the land
His Wessex reigned supreme. He is remembered –
Sword aloft in Winchester he stands.

The Saxon church of Sherborne was enveloped
By Norman masons, making nave and choir
Of Cotswold stone, whose climbing fans uphold
The roof embossed. When tyranny reached out,
Stubborn townsmen stumped up ready cash
To keep the church their own, so that today
We roam the aisles to read our history
In stone.
         But, in the north aisle by the choir,
Two slabs are taken up. Conveniently for curious tourists
A switch provides a light, for them to peer
Inside the broken tomb, where there are bones –
King Ethelbald, King Ethelred, on view –
I'm sorry that I pressed that switch. Don't they
Deserve the decent privacy of a tomb?

1987   *Marjorie Baker*

INDEX OF POETS